Gordon B. Hinckley
Fifteenth President of the Church

Gordon B. Hinckley
Fifteenth President of the Church

Melinda T. Garff

Illustrated by Robert T. Barrett

Bookcraft
Salt Lake City, Utah

For Alicia, Skyler, Janelle, and Laura—MTG

For Vicki and the kids—RTB

Library of Congress Catalog Card Number: 98-73239
ISBN 1-57008-534-X

First Printing, 1998

Printed in the United States of America

"I never want to travel anywhere again!" said twenty-five-year-old Gordon B. Hinckley as he returned home from Europe. Little did he know that in the years ahead he would spend a great deal of time traveling all over the world as a great leader in The Church of Jesus Christ of Latter-day Saints.

On June 23, 1910, Gordon Bitner Hinckley, the first child of Ada Bitner Hinckley and Bryant S. Hinckley, was born in Salt Lake City.

As a child Gordon was not very healthy. He had problems with earaches and allergies, and he was very sick with whooping cough when he was two years old. Doctors told his parents that he needed lots of fresh country air in order to get better. So Gordon's father bought some farmland in an area of Salt Lake called East Millcreek.

When they weren't at the farm in East Millcreek, Gordon's family lived in this home in downtown Salt Lake. Gordon and his friends in Salt Lake would play kick the can and marbles, and in winter they would sled, skate, and play fox and geese.

The Hinckley family would spend their summers and some holidays and weekends on the farm. There Gordon and his brothers and sisters learned to work hard and play hard. They would jump off of haystacks, gather eggs, weed the garden, and do many other outdoor activities.

One of Gordon's favorite things to do was to sleep in a wagon box out under the stars during the summer. He learned to identify some of the constellations and became particularly interested in the North Star, which did not change positions the way other stars did. The North Star was constant and dependable, and that is the kind of person Gordon would become.

Gordon was especially close to his brother Sherman, who was just sixteen months younger than Gordon.

Soon Gordon was old enough to attend school, but he didn't want to go. On the first day, he tried to hide from his parents so that he wouldn't have to go.

As Gordon grew older, he learned to like school. He enjoyed the classes in which he was able to work with tools. He was good at building and fixing things. When he was older he would build his own home.

Gordon also liked to read and to learn about history. Both of Gordon's parents had been teachers, and they wanted their children to love books and learning. So one room in the Hinckley home became a library with over one thousand books in it.

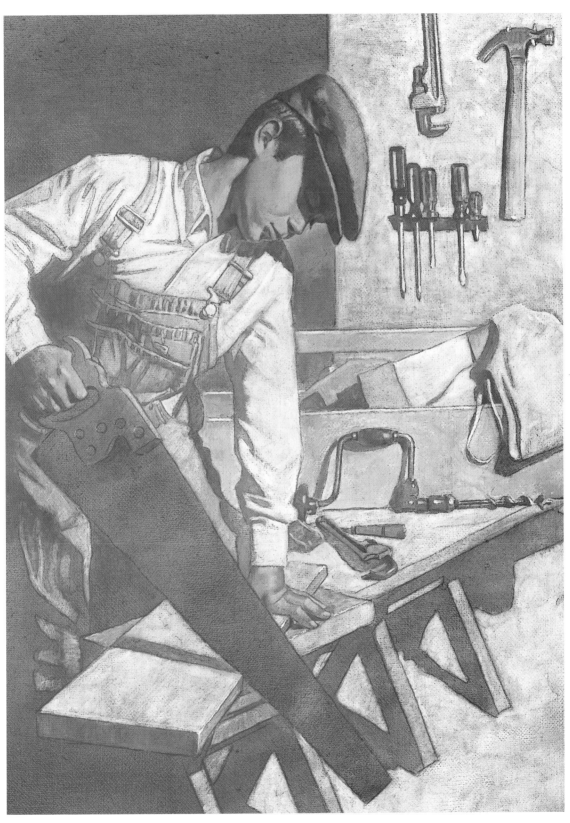

Gordon and Sherman both liked to work with tools. They would make things such as doll furniture for their sisters, household items for their mother, and "inventions" of all types.

When Gordon was in the seventh grade he and some of his friends protested a school decision by skipping classes one day. As a result, the principal said that before the boys would be allowed to return to school, each of them would have to bring him a note from their parents. Gordon's mother was not happy about her son's action. She wrote to the principal: "Dear Mr. Stearns, Please excuse Gordon's absence yesterday. His action was simply an impulse to follow the crowd."

Gordon did not want to be known as someone who would just "follow the crowd." He decided that he should always do what was right, no matter what situation he was in.

When Gordon was in elementary school the boys wore shirts, ties, short trousers, and long black stockings that reached to above their knees. They were required to look neat and tidy for school.

Gordon's parents also wanted their children to grow up to be good people who loved the Lord. Together the family read the scriptures, attended Church meetings, and held family home evenings. From his experiences at home and from his parents' example, young Gordon began to see how important the Church really was.

Gordon's feelings about the Church became even stronger when he was twelve years old. As a newly ordained deacon he attended his first stake priesthood meeting with his father. During that meeting all of the men and boys stood and sang the hymn about the Prophet Joseph Smith called "Praise to the Man." As they sang, Gordon felt in his heart "the conviction that Joseph Smith was a prophet of God." From that day on, this testimony never left Gordon.

"Praise to the Man," a hymn about the Prophet Joseph Smith, had a powerful influence on twelve-year-old Gordon B. Hinckley. Gordon's father thought of Joseph Smith and the other Church Presidents as his heroes. These great men became Gordon's heroes also.

When he was older Gordon attended college at the University of Utah. He earned a degree in English, and he wanted to continue going to school and study journalism. Those plans changed when in 1933 he was called to serve a mission in England. Because of the worldwide depression, Gordon and his family did not have much money, but even so they agreed he should go on this mission.

To get to England to serve his mission, Gordon first traveled by train from Salt Lake City to New York City. There he boarded a big steamship called the MANHATTAN. It took the ship about a week to cross the Atlantic Ocean and arrive in England.

During the first part of his mission Gordon felt lonely and discouraged. He thought that he was wasting his time and his father's money, and he wanted to go home. When he wrote and told his father these things, his father sent back a letter that said: "Dear Gordon, I have your recent letter. I have only one suggestion: forget yourself and go to work." Gordon decided that this was what he needed to do. He later said: "I count that as the day of decision in my life. Everything good that has happened to me since then I can trace back to the decision I made at that time."

The rest of his mission experiences helped Gordon learn some important lessons that would stay with him all his life. He learned to be positive and trust in the Lord, even when things were difficult. He learned to speak up and defend the Church. And he learned that serving the Lord is rewarding.

While serving in London, on Sundays Gordon and the other missionaries took turns holding "street meetings" in parks in the city. These outdoor gatherings included singing, prayer, and preaching.

After his mission Gordon was asked by President David O. McKay, then a counselor to President Heber J. Grant, to work as the secretary of a committee of the Council of the Twelve Apostles. So Gordon again gave up the idea of going back to college and began to work for the Church. As part of his job, Gordon wrote many Church materials and radio programs. He also taught seminary for a while.

Many of the materials Gordon helped create were used in missionary work. When the Church decided to put an exhibit in the 1939 World's Fair, Gordon came up with the idea to make a replica of the Salt Lake Tabernacle. Thousands of people visited this exhibit and learned about the Church.

During his early working years, in the spring of 1937, Gordon married Marjorie Pay in the Salt Lake Temple. Gordon and Marjorie first met years before, when they were children in Primary. Back then Marjorie had given readings, and Gordon remembered one particular reading she gave. "I don't know what it did to me, but I never forgot it. Then she grew older into a beautiful young woman, and I had the good fortune to marry her."

During the first few years of their marriage, Gordon and Marjorie lived in the farm home in East Millcreek—the same home Gordon had spent summers in as a boy. The home needed a furnace for winter, and so Gordon installed one himself.

The Hinckleys had five children: Kathleen, Richard, Virginia, Clark, and Jane. Growing up in the Hinckley family was a lot of fun. Gordon loved a good joke or story. At dinnertime he would often tell his family a funny story he had heard at work. He would start to laugh, and sometimes he laughed so hard that his face would turn red and he almost couldn't breathe.

For family vacations the Hinckleys sometimes traveled outside of Utah, but they often stayed within the state. Gordon and Marjorie wanted their children to appreciate Church history and their pioneer ancestors, so as they traveled they would stop at every historical marker they could find.

On vacations Marjorie would read to the family in the car. One time she read Where the Red Fern Grows, *and when she finished, everyone was crying. Though they had reached their vacation spot, they had to stay in the car and drive around until everyone had stopped crying.*

In April 1958 President McKay called
Gordon B. Hinckley to be a General Authority.
In the years that followed, Elder Hinckley went
to many places all over the world. He did not
really like to travel, but he loved the people he
met and appreciated all that he learned. As he
traveled he helped find land and make plans
for many meetinghouses and temples.

Over the years, Elder Hinckley worked
in one way or another with eight Presidents of
the Church—from Heber J. Grant to Howard W.
Hunter. He served as a counselor to three of
these great men: Spencer W. Kimball, Ezra Taft
Benson, and Howard W. Hunter. As these
prophets grew older and had many health
problems, President Hinckley had to take on
great responsibilities in the Church.

As a Church leader President Hinckley has
been involved with the building of temples. In
fact, he has dedicated more than half of the
temples in use around the globe.

During temple dedications, President Hinckley has often taken part in the cornerstone ceremony, which includes applying a bit of mortar with a tool called a trowel. Concerning the construction of temples around the world, he has said, "We are living in the greatest era of temple building ever witnessed."

After working and serving in the Church for sixty years, Gordon B. Hinckley was ordained and set apart as prophet and President of The Church of Jesus Christ of Latter-day Saints on March 12, 1995. Though he is no longer a young man, he keeps a busy schedule. He continues to travel over the world, showing his love for and interest in the people of the Church. Every group of people he visits feels as if they are his favorite people.

In February 1998 President Hinckley traveled to Africa. He met many Church members there, including Primary children. President Hinckley was the first Church President to visit West Africa.

President Hinckley often meets with important persons in the United States and other countries. His sense of humor, his great knowledge of many subjects, and his love of people help him to be comfortable with anyone, whether it be the president of the United States or a new Church member in a far-off country.

Through his words and by his example, President Hinckley has taught the members of the Church many important principles. Some of these are that we need to
    —work at creating strong, righteous families
    —be positive and look for the good in life
    —put our trust in the Lord
    —spend more time learning and reading
      good books and less time watching T.V.
    —do our best in whatever situation we may
      be in

Beginning with his boyhood experiences and continuing on throughout his life, President Hinckley has been prepared for the great calling he now holds. He has said that he would like to be remembered "as a man who tried to do some good in the world," and that is exactly what he has done. As a humble servant of the Lord he has traveled the world, bringing hope, leaving love, and doing good.